Odell Mitchell Jr.

▶ **RECONQUERED**

Twilight gleams on the Missouri and Mississippi rivers, united in mid-July 1993 20 miles upstream of their usual confluence.

One who knows the Mississippi will promptly aver — not aloud but to himself — that ten thousand River Commissions, with the mines of the world at their back, cannot tame that lawless stream, cannot curb it or confine it, cannot say to it, "Go here," or "Go there," and make it obey; cannot save a shore which it has sentenced; cannot bar its path with an obstruction which it will not tear down, dance over, and laugh at.

▶ *Mark Twain*, **Life on the Mississippi**

Karen Elshout

▶ **UPROOTED**

Debby Westfall carries her five-year-old son, Jesse, while her husband, Dale, tows some of their belongings from the subdivision where they lived in northern St. Charles County. At the flood's peak, a third of the county was underwater.

To the victims, and the volunteers

As this book goes to press, the Mississippi River is still above flood stage in St. Louis. The water has fallen dramatically and steadily, but beyond the broken levees, in valleys and low-lying fields, there are lagoons still. Many homes and businesses remain uninhabitable. The toll in human misery and economic loss continues to increase.

St. Louis — and the entire Midwest — had never seen or experienced anything like the Great Flood of '93. At one point, the waters from the Mississippi, the Missouri and their tributaries covered 15,600 square miles, an area greater than the size of Lake Erie or Lake Ontario.

The victims of the flood numbered in the tens of thousands. Up and down the rivers, some 55,000 homes were damaged or destroyed. The cost of the damage was estimated at $10 billion to $15 billion. Fifty people died, 30 of them in Missouri and Illinois.

But even as the suffering intensified and spread, a wonderful thing began to take place. Thousands upon thousands of volunteers materialized, to take in the newly homeless, to provide a meal or clean clothes or to replace a child's ruined toy. Most of all, the volunteers turned out to sandbag.

They came in all ages, all colors, and all sizes. Anonymous, heedless of fatigue or the clock, they filled and hoisted and heaved sandbags, millions of them, and if the levees were overwhelmed, as the levees frequently were, they went on to the next one. They saved small cottages and entire towns alike. And St. Louis — and the entire Midwest — had never seen anything like that, either.

▶ **SENTINELS**

Sandbags await duty in Kimmswick, a historic hamlet on the Mississippi 25 miles south of St. Louis. A volunteer-built earth and sandbag wall saved most of the town's restored buildings.

To the victims and the volunteers, and the men and women of the Post-Dispatch who took their pictures and told their stories, *High and Mighty: The Flood of '93* is dedicated. By itself, this contribution will not nearly meet the need. But we think of it as our own special sandbag, and we are proud of the effort that went into it.

William F. Woo
Editor
St. Louis Post-Dispatch

▶ **SWEPT AWAY** *(Cover photo)*

Its protective levee saturated, then ripped asunder, a farm near Columbia, Ill., succumbs to floodwater from the swollen Mississippi.

HIGH AND MIGHTY

THE FLOOD OF '93

Kevin Manning

▶ **WATERWAY**

At the flood's peak on Aug. 1, more than 1,080,000 cubic feet of water rushed past the Gateway Arch in St. Louis every second — probably the highest ever recorded, hydrologists said.

ST. LOUIS POST-DISPATCH

Photographs by the staff of the St. Louis Post-Dispatch
Text by Virgil Tipton
Editing by Susan Clotfelter
Design and layout by Tony Lazorko and J. B. Forbes
Supervising editor: Ron Willnow

ANDREWS AND MCMEEL
A Universal Press Syndicate Company
KANSAS CITY

Library of Congress Cataloging-in-Publication Data

High and mighty : the flood of 1993 / by the staff of the St. Louis
   post-dispatch.
       p.   cm.
    ISBN 0-8362-8047-4 : $12.95
     1. Floods—Mississippi River Valley—History—20th century.
  2. Floods—Missouri River Valley—History—20th century. 3. Floods—
 ⁻Mississippi River Valley—Pictorial works. 4. Floods—Missouri
 River Valley—Pictorial works. 5. Mississippi River Valley—
 ⁻History—1865- 6. Missouri River Valley—History. 7. Mississippi
 River Valley—Pictorial works. 8. Missouri River Valley—Pictorial
 works. I. St. Louis post-dispatch.
 F472.M6H54 1993
 977'.033—dc20   93-36313
                                                                 CIP

ATTENTION: SCHOOLS AND BUSINESSES

Andrews and McMeel books are available at quantity discounts with bulk purchase for educational, business, or sales promotional use. For information, please write to: Special Sales Department, Andrews and McMeel, 4900 Main Street, Kansas City, Missouri 64112.

Scott Dine

▶ **SEVERED**

The Missouri River swallows the approach to a bridge in Washington, Mo. The flood not only hampered road traffic, causing hundred-mile detours, but closed the Mississippi to barges for months and briefly cut rail connections between St. Louis and Kansas City.

All proceeds received by the St. Louis Post-Dispatch from the sale of this book are being donated to flood relief. The St. Louis Post-Dispatch gratefully acknowledges the efforts of its staff who made this book and the contribution to flood relief possible.

Contents

A disaster of vast scope and stately pace

In the summer of 1993, the Midwest's rivers broke loose — and with them, all hell.

As the Mississippi and Missouri rivers heaved to record heights, they twisted landscape and lives out of shape in nine states. Powered by relentless rain, the slow-motion disaster rolled over at least 15,600 square miles, killed 50 people, damaged or destroyed 55,000 homes, stole at least 30,000 jobs and wreaked billions of dollars worth of damage.

The rivers engulfed homes up to their roofs, threatened historic settlements that had stayed dry for centuries, peeled slabs of concrete from roadbeds and elbowed into a high-tech business zone just hours after officials had declared it safe. Time after time, the flood ravaged what had once been considered untouchable — cherished churches, prisons, airports, urban neighborhoods and country schools.

At its most macabre, the flood carved into a cemetery and dragged hundreds of caskets and burial vaults miles downstream.

The size of this flood astonished even people who had made careers of watching the rivers. Just a month before the Mississippi surged to its high point of 49.58 feet at St. Louis, river forecasters predicted that the river would rise no higher than 40 feet.

The difference between the prediction and the reality was the difference between water at the doorstep and water up to the eaves.

■

Because of its leisurely pace, a Midwestern flood resembles no other natural disaster. It seems to savor destruction. An earthquake or a hurricane snaps at a town and is done with it. But a flood slinks into a river valley and feeds on it for days, for weeks, or, as in this case, for months. Or a flood can loiter maddeningly, then suddenly explode through a levee.

Imagine an earthquake hits your town, but that it rumbles for weeks instead of seconds. A crack in the earth snakes toward your house at a snail's pace. You see it coming and you know that, if it hits, it will break your home in half. But will it hit or will it veer away in time? Will it suddenly retreat? Can you do anything to stop it?

That's how the flood gnawed at its victims in the Mississippi and Missouri valleys.

A wall of caramel-colored water soaked levees and sandbag walls in St. Charles County for weeks while volunteers scrambled to reinforce them. And then the water swatted the barriers aside, one after another.

Water crawled through farmland in Pike County for days, then swallowed a school eight miles from the Mississippi River's normal course — minutes after sandbaggers gave up.

In St. Louis, where the Mississippi shoved backwater into a tributary called the River Des Peres, a wall of sandbags teetered for days and then collapsed.

And after floodwater conquered a valley, the victims could do nothing but wait for the water to recede before going back home. Some would never be able to return.

In the midst of the flood, building inspectors hopped into boats and toured flooded homes in Lemay.

"Some you can look at and tell there are problems already," said Jim White, St. Louis County's emergency chief.

"They're collapsing."

■

Sometimes, people won.

In Prairie du Rocher, a hamlet that calls itself the oldest continuous town in Illinois, an absurd and desperate plan worked: Townspeople intentionally broke open a levee to save their town.

Sam Leone

In Hannibal, Mark Twain's hometown, a flood wall kept downtown dry. In St. Louis, the flood wall protecting low spots in the city restrained the Mississippi, even though the wall was weakened by a hole underneath. And dozens of levees guarding homes and farmland held firm, although the rivers had eaten countless holes in them.

Thousands of volunteers helped fight the flood, 10,000 in St. Charles County alone. They walked or drove or flew to the flood zone so they could shovel sand, heft sandbags, serve food, save animals or rescue people. They worked in 90-degree heat for hours or days. They worked without reward.

Maybe that was a victory too.

"It's good for your soul," said volunteer sandbagger Susan Zwygart. "It also makes you cry."

Lethargic though a flood may be, it wields vast power — vast enough to topple trees too big to wrap your arms around, vast enough to crumple a bridge like a discarded lunch bag.

But despite its power, there is no malice in the river.

▶ **REFUGEE**

A fawn inches across a swamped Missouri River levee in St. Charles County in July. While deer, raccoons and other wild animals fled flooded bottomland, egrets and other normally scarce wading birds began reappearing in the river's reclaimed flood plain.

The Mississippi River and its sibling, the Missouri, have nurtured humans for millennia, since the first explorers crossed the Bering land bridge into North America. The remnants of Native American settlements still mark the bluffs along the rivers.

Centuries later, the rivers' resources drew French, Spanish and English settlers, fur trappers, riverboat pilots, farmers, merchants and soldiers. The rivers inspired artists, architects and writers. They bore the nation's commerce, long before we built highways.

And the rivers flooded, as they have done for hundreds of thousands of years. The bluffs — the borders marking where the rivers have carved into the earth — show by the distance between them how far the rivers have spread from their banks.

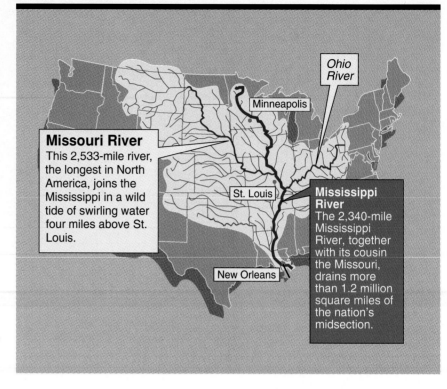

Missouri River
This 2,533-mile river, the longest in North America, joins the Mississippi in a wild tide of swirling water four miles above St. Louis.

Mississippi River
The 2,340-mile Mississippi River, together with its cousin the Missouri, drains more than 1.2 million square miles of the nation's midsection.

A flood is a river's way of cleansing itself. Like a garden hose sprayed on a driveway, a flood carries sand and silt and debris out of the riverbed. When the water slides away from the flood plain, it usually leaves behind a layer of silt that enriches the land.

A river's flood is not really a disaster; it's merely part of a long cycle in the river's life, as natural as your breathing. The disaster was that we got in the way.

Why?

Barriers like flood walls and levees let farmers, manufacturers and developers go about their business without a yearly deluge. The success of those barriers for decades encouraged more barriers, and more development beyond farmhouses and fields. Too much development, some people warned.

Constricting a river simply pushes the floodwater somewhere else. In big floods, when the water has nowhere else to go, levees and other barriers split open, like buttons popping off a shrunken shirt.

This flood smashed records as well as levees. At 10 a.m. on Aug. 1, the Mississippi roared past St. Louis higher than ever recorded — 49.58 feet, or 19.58 feet above flood stage and three dozen feet higher than its normal mid-summer flow. The crest — the flood's high point

— was more than 6 feet higher than the old record, set in 1973.

Hydrologists measure a river from a point somewhere above the riverbed, around 12 feet in the case of the Mississippi at St. Louis. That's because the riverbed shifts over the years, making an unreliable starting point. What all that means is that a river coursing by at a level of 49 feet is actually more like 61 feet deep — about six stories.

At the flood's peak, more than 1,080,000 cubic feet of water — 8.1 million gallons — charged past the Gateway Arch every second. If you collected one second's flow in plastic jugs, you'd have enough to give every man, woman and child in Missouri a gallon of river water, with 2 1/2 million gallons to spare. If you let the tap run for a minute and 7 seconds, you'd fill Busch Stadium to the flagpoles.

At St. Charles, the Missouri climbed to 39.6 feet about 10 p.m. on Aug. 2. That mark was 14.6 feet above flood stage and 2.1 feet above the old record, set in 1986.

Both of the rivers flooded to or beyond what hydrologists call the "100-year" level. That's a flood so big that it carries only a 1 in 100 chance of happening in any year. But now that 100-year floods have passed, that doesn't

mean that people living in the flood plains can relax for 99 years.

"When the year ends, the slate is erased," said Gary Dyhouse, a hydrologist with the Army Corps of Engineers. "We start all over again, at a 1 percent chance."

By the time the Mississippi's crest had swept past Cairo and into history, people upstream had trudged into the second phase of the flood — the cleanup. People who had lived for weeks or months in spartan shelters or who had crammed into houses with friends returned to find their homes pasted with mud, garbage and human waste.

"We've got dead fish on the streets and a lot of debris," said Bellefontaine Neighbors Mayor Marty Rudloff. "And it's starting to smell really, really bad."

From its birth in the sky miles above the Midwest, to its skirmishes with volunteers along desperate sandbag lines, to its end in dank homes heavy with loss, this is the story of the flood of 1993.

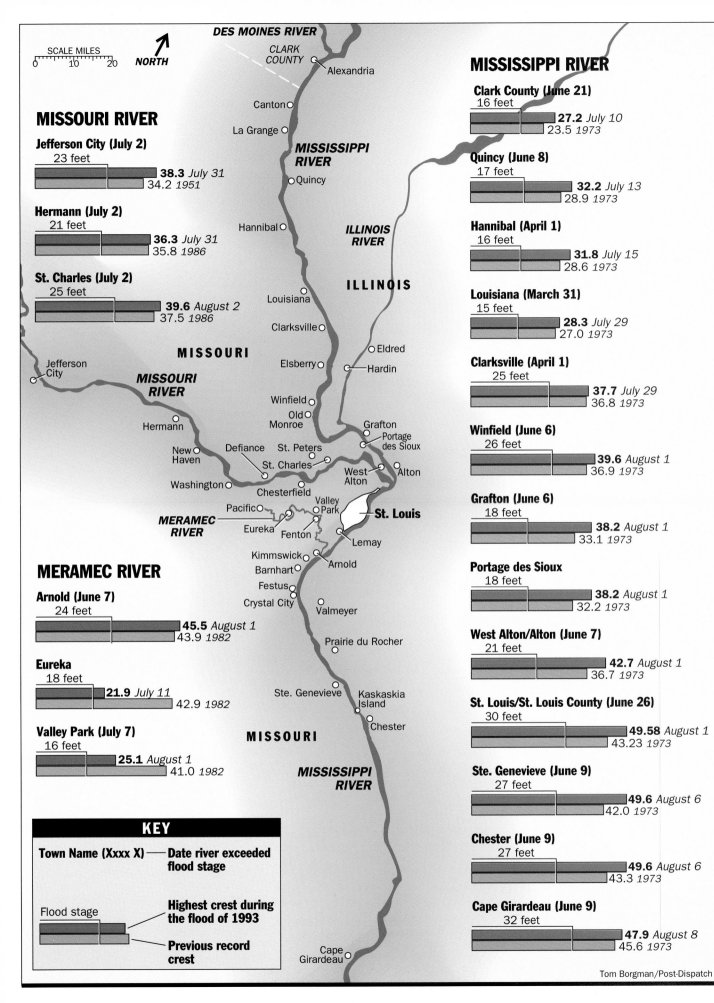

Signs in the skies and streams

The flood began innocently enough — with a squiggle in the air currents over North America.

Normally, the upper-level river of air called the jet stream flows northward into Canada in the summer. But in the summer of 1993, the stream dipped inexplicably into the Midwest and stayed put. Like a boot pinning a snake, it trapped weather systems in place over North America, and those systems spun out storms that lashed the upper Mississippi Valley.

Rain fell and fell and fell. In one month, some spots in Missouri and Iowa absorbed five times their normal amount of rainfall. Those downpours sloshed into streams already brimming with spring rainfall; the streams pumped billions of gallons into bigger rivers, which emptied that water into the Missouri and Mississippi rivers.

"That water has to go somewhere," meteorologist Dave Metze of the National Weather Service said in the flood's early days. "And where it will go is downstream. We're downstream."

In the beginning, the flood swamped farmland and small river towns accustomed to flooding. At the St. Louis riverfront, the Mississippi rose beyond its normal summer level and crept over a cobblestone bank and toward a street. But that didn't faze St. Louisans. No flood had seriously threatened St. Louis in decades.

As the summer dragged on, the saturated ground could take no more water. Rain that normally would have soaked into the earth slid into streams. The river forecasters were befuddled. They would change their predictions for river levels daily. And they'd still be wrong.

Meanwhile, floodwater started to rise onto highways and into homes long thought inviolable.

Renyold Ferguson

▶ **FIRST WAVES**

In April, barricades on Leonor K. Sullivan Boulevard became superfluous as three straight days of rain pounded St. Louis, poured off saturated lawns and filled storm sewers, rendering St. Louis' main riverfront street impassable.

In Des Moines, Iowa, flooded rivers engulfed the city's water plant. About 250,000 people endured nine days without clean water. Residents used pool water to flush toilets; they captured rainwater in buckets.

In northwestern Missouri, floods severed the water supply for nearly 100,000 people.

Near Jefferson City, Mo., the Missouri River closed highways linking the capital with the northern half of the state and even chewed one section into rubble. It toppled a railroad bridge. It yanked a 16,000-gallon propane tank off its mount and split it open, venting explosive gas.

In Ray County in western Missouri, the Missouri sliced into a cemetery and floated vaults downstream. "The morti-

Scott Dine

INUNDATED ◀

A farm near Winfield, Mo., gradually loses more and more of its crop to the Mississippi in July.

Chronology:

▶ **March 5, 1993:**

After a wet winter, the Mississippi Valley faces a wet spring. In a preview of what's to come, the Mississippi at St. Louis rises 14 feet in 48 hours. The Missouri River at Hermann rises 11 feet in 48 hours

▶ **March 16:**

The National Weather Service predicts that the Ohio Valley may face flooding in the spring because of the March 13 blizzard.

▶ **April 14:**

Because of heavy rainfall, only 2 percent of Missouri's corn crop is planted, the worst record in almost a decade.

In the Orchard Farm School District in St. Charles County, Tabitha and Brandy Brown go to school a new way — by boating to their bus stop.

In St. Louis, the Mississippi crawls above a cobblestone riverbank and crosses Leonor K. Sullivan Boulevard.

▶ **April 16:**

To date, St. Louis has soaked up 13.03 inches of rain, about four inches more than normal. The Mississippi touches the bottom step on the Gateway Arch's staircase.

▶ **April 17:**

The Mississippi drives some residents of Grafton from their homes.

▶ **April 22:**

Illinois Gov. Jim Edgar declares Grafton a disaster area. Meanwhile, residents roam through their homes in knee-high wading boots–what they call "Grafton tennis shoes."

cians tell me that the newer vaults are sealed, so as soon as the water washes the dirt off of them, they pop up just like a balloon," said Don Blankenship, the acting police chief in Hardin, Mo.

The Mississippi swamped approaches to bridges linking Illinois with Missouri, forcing commuters in small towns north and south of St. Louis into 100-mile detours to cross the river.

And in Chester, Ill., the river choked the water supply to Menard Correctional Center, a maximum security prison. The 2,450 inmates could neither flush toilets nor take showers. Warden George Welborn's reaction would become a common sentiment:

"We've got some serious problems. And the damned water just keeps coming."

J.B. Forbes

▶ UNDAUNTED

In an early July downpour, neighbors gather in Portage des Sioux for a feast of crawfish that the flooded Mississippi dumped on Highway 94. They didn't believe that the river would reach their house — but by the flood's end, the river was flowing through it.

▼ FORESHADOWED

Dawn Boschert of Portage des Sioux sizes up the oncoming storm from Highway 94. By June's end, the state of Missouri had received 8 inches more than a whole normal year's 19 inches of precipitation.

Scott Dine

▼ AMPHIBIAN

A truck motors upstream through encroaching Illinois River water on the state's Highway 100. Like St. Charles County in Missouri, Illinois' Calhoun County sits between two rivers.

Larry Williams

▶ **CORRALLED**

Coast Guard officers and Humane Society workers round up cattle on a farm near Alton. Some farmers moved livestock to higher ground in time; others lost animals from cats to catfish.

Farmers: The first to fall

Jerry Huber clenched his jaw as he looked over the brown lake that once had been green fields rustling with his corn and beans. Like a punchline in some cosmic joke, a muskrat swam by.

"Farming was the thing I always wanted to do," Huber said. "That's all I did from the time I was old enough to walk, sitting up on the tractor with my dad. I never thought I would see the water this high. Never."

As the flood scoured the Mississippi and Missouri river valleys, its first victims were farmers in the flood plains. When the water finally receded, it unveiled rotting crops and fields that would stay sodden for weeks.

Throughout the Midwest, water either flooded 7.1 million acres of farm-

land or left them too wet to plant, the U.S. Department of Agriculture said. That's 11,000 square miles — an area as big as a fifth of Illinois, or Vermont with a couple of Rhode Islands thrown in. The department's price for the flood and the summer's drought: $2.5 billion in lost soybean and corn crops alone. That leaves out damaged tractors, silos and barns and drowned livestock.

"We lost all our chickens," said farmer Wayne Bienfang, who lives near Minneapolis. "All our pheasants. All drowned. We got some of the pigs out. Two of them got stuck where I couldn't get to them, and the water was coming up, and I had to shoot them."

On the day Huber scanned his flooded field, the rivers were still two weeks from reaching their crests in the St. Louis area. Even veteran farmers shook their heads.

"No man alive has seen this much water," said farmer Donny Dunkmann.

Sam Leone

▼

THWARTED

A few lonely stalks peek above the Missouri River from Jerry Huber's cornfields.

Chronology:

▶ **April 27:**
Lock and Dam 25 at Winfield shuts down because of spring floods, stranding some barges upriver.

▶ **April 28:**
Gov. Mel Carnahan declares a state of emergency in St. Charles County, where thousands of acres of farmland already are flooded.

▶ **May 1:**
St. Charles County officials set up a portable shower in a parking lot in West Alton. It's for flood victims who are living in homes without working plumbing.

▶ **May 11:**
President Bill Clinton authorizes federal aid for flood victims in St. Charles and Lincoln counties.

▶ **May 29:**
A dry week lets some Missouri and Illinois farmers plant a few fields, but 5,000 acres in St. Charles County still have water standing in them.

▶ **June 25:**
The Army Corps of Engineers in St. Louis warns that rain in the north will cause flooding here. The Coast Guard closes a 215-mile stretch of the Mississippi River from Canton, Mo., to Bellevue, Iowa.

▶ **June 27:**
The Mississippi creeps back above flood level in St. Louis.

MAROONED *(Preceding pages)*

An inland sea surrounds a farm in north St. Charles County in early July. Even farmers on high ground were hurt as diseases, weeds and insects flourished in the soaked soil and moist air.

Wayne Crosslin

Wayne Crosslin

NEIGHBORS ◀

Floodwater connects two farm homes in rural Portage des Sioux, near the confluence of the Mississippi and Missouri rivers.

▶ STRICKEN

A barn belonging to Art Benne of St. Charles County burned to its waterline after it was hit by lightning in August.

Karen Elshout

Odell Mitchell Jr.

Kaskaskia Island residents reclaim one of many stray pigs from along the island's ruptured levee in late July. "We got them off of rooftops and off houses and trees," said farmer Dan Lankford. "I don't know how they hung on, but they did. They'd swim to a tree and hang over a limb."

Stranded where the waters meet

S*creeeeeech.* Something scraped at the bottom of the National Guard raft as it skimmed over the brown lake that used to be northern St. Charles County. Sunburned and drenched in sweat, Sgt. Lonnie Salts leaned over and peered into the water to see what the obstacle was.

It was a road sign: "West Alton 9 miles."

In the century's biggest flood in the lower Midwest, St. Charles County had the bad luck to be pinched between the nation's two mightiest rivers: the Mississippi and Missouri. In the flood of 1993, water as deep as 20 feet roiled over a third of the county — 200 square miles.

The county, northwest of St. Louis,

has long glowed with the light of promise because of the rivers. Early settlers told themselves that this prime location, not St. Louis, would grow into the region's commercial hub. The city of St. Charles served as Missouri's first capital. Regular floods had lavished silt on the nearby fields, creating some of the richest farmland in the country.

Today the county blends Missouri's past and present: huge family farms, archetypal rural towns, high-tech defense plants and tony riverfront boutiques. In the last decade, no Missouri county has grown faster.

But in 1993, the rivers became the enemy.

In St. Charles County, the flood

evicted 10,000 people, demolished levee after levee and swallowed thousands of acres of farmland and hundreds of homes. The Mississippi and Missouri rivers, bloated by three wet seasons, merged 20 miles upstream of their usual meeting point.

By the time the rivers rolled to their crests, they had inundated Defiance, Portage des Sioux, West Alton, Orchard Farm and other small towns, and had even reached into the northern tip of St. Charles, the county's biggest city.

In a flood-stricken state, St. Charles County was the most flooded county.

"It's a worst-case scenario," Gary Schuchardt, the county's emergency management chief, said in the midst of the flood. "And probably beyond that."

The county's major levee — a 23-mile earthen berm running between St.

Jerry Naunheim Jr.

CONSOLATION

The Rev. Donald E. Rau, pastor of St. Francis of Assisi Church in Portage des Sioux, catches a ride across the flooded town with the help of Coast Guardsmen Tom Jasina (left) and Bill Doerr. That Sunday, a week before the flood's crest, Rau came to say Mass for 20 parishioners in the town's historic church.

Despite those trials, some people stayed in their homes, surrounded by brown water. In Portage des Sioux, the few dozen remaining residents shopped, visited friends and picked up mail — all in waist-deep water. Or they packed appliances and pets into canoes and towed them to high ground. "It's like Venice," a Coast Guard officer said.

As floodwater stretched toward St. Francis of Assisi Catholic Church, a landmark since 1879 and a symbol of the town's resilience, residents despaired. The residents and the St. Louis Archdiocese let a team from Mississippi Tarp Co. in Meridian, Miss., wrap the church in plastic to keep its foundation dry.

It didn't work.

At the peak of the flooding, the Mississippi and the Missouri violated the church's sanctuary, buckled flooring in the center aisle and lapped at the seats of the wooden pews.

Even after that defeat, the holdouts stayed.

In mid-July, when Salts and other National Guard soldiers rafted into Portage des Sioux on a mission to clear out whichever townspeople wanted to leave, a town official told them everyone wanted to stay.

Resident Steve Hopkins explained it this way: "Everybody's more or less resigned to it. Old Man River did what he wanted to do."

Charles and West Alton — tore open July 16 as volunteer sandbaggers and residents tried to reinforce it. Even after the break, a handful of residents desperately flung sandbags at the advance, and gave up only after the water had reached their knees.

From then on, levees failed about every other day. By late July, emergency workers realized that whatever could flood already had. "There isn't much levee left," said Petra Haws, a spokeswoman for the county's emergency crews.

Bizarrely, at the flood's peak, three tornadoes blasted through St. Charles County. Two touched down in the flood-stricken towns of St. Peters and Portage des Sioux. The tornadoes themselves caused little damage, but the wind kicked up 3-foot waves that chewed some homes to pieces.

▶ **BECALMED**

North of the city of St. Charles, an evacuated mobile home park sits in eerie isolation.

▼

BURDENED

West Alton flood victims ferry belongings under a railroad trestle near Missouri Highway 94. The town sits closest to the normal confluence of the Mississippi and Missouri rivers.

Jerry Naunheim Jr.   Sam Leone

▶ **COVERED**

Even headstones in the cemetery of St. Francis of Assisi Church in Portage des Sioux take on their share of the floodwater in late July.

PENNED ◀

Surrounded by water, Carl Zimmerman's four dogs find refuge on the roof of his two-story house near Harbor Point in St. Charles County. Many flood victims had to leave pets behind; few emergency shelters could accept them and few hotels would.

Sam Leone

RETRIEVED

After the photograph of the labrador-mix dogs stranded on a roof appeared in the St. Louis Post-Dispatch, phone calls flooded the newspaper. Lisa Thess of the Pet Adoption Center of St. Charles, with help from the Missouri Water Patrol, moved the dogs to higher ground and tried to contact Zimmerman. One of the dogs turned out to be pregnant; another young puppy was still nursing.

Renyold Ferguson

J.B. Forbes

GROUNDED ◄

Like feeding livestock, small planes line up at the waterline at the county's Smartt Field. Many owners moved their aircraft to the Spirit of St. Louis Airport in Chesterfield, which later flooded as well.

▼
LEFTOVERS

Sated for the time being, Craig Vogt, Pat Weber and Kevin Machens of Portage des Sioux return surplus crawfish to the Mississippi a few feet from their garage door.

Wes Paz

▼ CRUMPLED

Family and friends of Herbert and Katharine Farley of West Alton inspect damage to the couple's grain storage buildings.

▶ TURNED OUT

Theresa and Scott Gluckhertz comfort one another as friends help them collect belongings in St. Charles Mobile Home Community.

Wendi Fitzgerald

OVERPOWERED

Bob Pinkley (front left), Roger Leesmann (front right) and others pull a boatload of pumps out of Terry and Betty's Tavern in the Missouri River hamlet of Defiance. The pumps kept the bar dry for a while after a levee broke there, but eventually the river won.

Kevin Manning

▼ SURROUNDED

Trucks from the St. Charles Quarry Co. fall in wheel-to-wheel on a patch of high ground near the Missouri River Aug. 2.

Scott Dine

Jim Rackwitz

Jerry Naunheim Jr.

INVADED ◄

Melissa Burckhardt's view from her flooded home in Portage des Sioux is of streets covered with chest-high water. Outside, her brother Jason, 19, inspects the river's work.

▼ OUTRIDER

Coast Guard Reserve Petty Officer Richard McComber, making rounds among mobile home residents near Portage des Sioux, checks in with Vance Virgin, Randy Witmore and Sheila Griffith. About 170 Coast Guard reservists helped patrol the St. Louis area during the flood; they came from as far away as Memphis and Leavenworth, Kan.

Tens of thousands of helping hands

As the flood rolled through the Midwest, volunteers rolled up their sleeves.

Tens of thousands of volunteers poured into the flood zone to shield homes they would never enter and to succor people they would never see again. They sacrificed lunch hours, evenings, weekends or vacations to shovel sand, fling sandbags, feed workers, operate radios and pump water. Or they donated clothes, food, money or room for refugees.

Their payment: sunburn, heat exhaustion, strained backs, blisters, aching muscles, slimmer wallets.

Ten thousand volunteers marched into St. Charles County alone. Sometimes, so many volunteers showed up after emergency crews broadcast a call for help that the crews had to send out another call soon afterward: That's enough!

No one kept a reliable count of volunteers. But emergency workers estimated their ranks in the tens of thousands, perhaps in the hundreds of thousands. Somehow, the Salvation Army, the American Red Cross and emergency agencies wrestled that stream into a mostly organized battle line. Workers from the Salvation Army and the Red Cross set up shelters, food lines and sandbag brigades and worked with emergency management agencies.

Meanwhile, rescuers from the national and local humane groups retrieved trapped pets and wildlife, and soldiers from the Army and Air National Guards sandbagged and patrolled evacuated neighborhoods. The Civil Air Patrol and amateur radio operators kept communication lines humming. In some spots, even prisoners volunteered — and worked.

James Rackwitz

▶ **APPRECIATION**

A hand-lettered sign at Virginia and Marceau Avenues near the River Des Peres. It, too, eventually succumbed to floodwater.

ayne Crosslin

MOBILIZED

Predictions of a new crest on the Mississippi July 16 drew hundreds of volunteers to the banks of the River Des Peres, a tributary creek that winds through the city's south neighborhoods and the suburb of Lemay. The volunteers toiled in heat above 90 degrees and stifling humidity to pile more sandbags on the already-saturated wall.

Jerry Naunheim Jr.

▶ **STALWART**

Frank Micklack stands in ankle-deep muck as if ready to single-handedly glare down the Mississippi in Kimmswick.

The volunteers came from next door, from the next state and from Australia and Germany.

The paid workers and the volunteers would fill in all the blanks — and more — on a census form. As volunteer Sue Bauer jokingly put it: "We've got white people, black people, gay people — and people from Effingham, Ill."

Jim Runyons, 41, worked at a couple of levees in St. Charles County, even with a back that surgeons had patched twice. "I feel like it's a hell of a cause," Runyons said. "So what's a back problem?"

Stacy Gruenloh, 20, gave up the last of her summer vacation to labor at a sandbag line in St. Charles. "The experience can change you," she said.

Dan Jarvis flew to St. Charles from Indianapolis to help. He flew because he has epilepsy and couldn't drive.

Conventioneers from the United Church of Christ, the Christian Church (Disciples of Christ) and the North American Christian Convention passed up seminars to work on sandbag lines.

Mike Leach of Tampa, Fla., was visiting relatives in Imperial when he heard about the flood. He worked in Kimm-

swick every day of his vacation. "Sure I'm tired," he said. "But it's worth it if it works."

And in Ste. Genevieve, Sunny Reed, 19, sandbagged for 32 hours straight.

"I got to be here because it's us against the river," Reed said. "We got to win."

VIGIL ◄

Volunteers keep the sandbags moving in south St. Louis at midnight, the night of the Mississippi's crest.

▼ FINISHING TOUCH

Sharae Gibbs, 5, tying sandbags near a threatened church in Festus. Children of all ages helped to fill and tie sandbags that in some cases outweighed them.

▼

UNFLINCHING *(Preceding pages)*

*City worker James Holt wades
across a levee break on the River
Des Peres July 21, in a stinging
rainstorm the day after the river
was supposed to have crested.
Mississippi backwater tossed aside
a mile-long stretch of sodden
sandbags that night in south St.
Louis. But that wasn't the worst
news: Equally heavy rains
upstream would send the river
heaving to new records a week
later.*

STEADFAST

Volunteers in Kimmswick work to secure plastic around a sandbag wall that protects the home of Brian Crow (far right) from the town's Rock Creek. Leaders of sandbag brigades quickly learned that, with the water likely to stay high, their walls were more durable when kept dry.

▶ WEDLOCKED

Missouri National Guard Spec. 4 Christine Schuler and Sgt. Robert Hurst put the final touch on their wedding ceremony Aug. 10 at the church in Crystal City where they were standing guard.

Renyold Ferguson

Jerry Naunheim Jr.

CKERED

stus street worker Matthew opst gets comfortable on the idwest's most ubiquitous item at summer; Charles Humphries hat) and Derrel Chaed prefer n-reclining seats.

Laying siege to the cities

A flying manhole cover can be a powerful convincer. Anyone who thought the flood of 1993 would spare metropolitan St. Louis thought otherwise when the steel lid spun through the air July 9 in Lemay.

Backwater from the Mississippi River and from Kayser Creek had filled the sewer lines, blasting the cover skyward. Water poured onto streets until workers could replace the lid and hold it down with sandbags.

It was just the beginning.

Over the following month, the Mississippi and Missouri rivers savaged large stretches of St. Louis and its suburbs.

The rivers engulfed more than 1,000 homes in St. Louis and St. Louis County, some up to their roof lines. Neighborhood streets swam with brown water and with scum-coated logs, tires, oil jugs and beer cans. The stink from sewage and rotting vegetation soured the air.

The flood shut four major bridges in the metropolitan area and closed two water plants. It swamped a sewage treatment plant, sending a river of raw sewage flowing past a wealthy enclave of St. Louis County.

Urban dwellers who live miles from the Missouri or Mississippi could have inflated a raft in their front yards and floated to the Gulf of Mexico.

In early July, the pessimistic saw hints that the Mississippi might stir things up in St. Louis. The VP Fair, the city's annual July 4 party, moved some of its rides to make way for the river, and the river forced the Casino Queen gambling boat to dock itself only three days after its maiden cruise.

City workers and volunteers started stacking sandbags along the River Des Peres levee, knowing that the Mississippi would shove backwater into that tributary. A few days after the sewer flipped its lid, police in south St. Louis told 1,000 people to move out. The news stunned residents.

"Never in my wildest dreams did I expect the river to come over its bank and come running down my street," Merlyn Bohler said as friends and relatives helped her pack.

On July 18, the flood hit hard.

The River Des Peres, suffocated with Mississippi backwater, shoved a section of sandbags from a levee, drowning dozens of homes.

"It started with a rumble in the ground, like a jet plane was going by," said Jeff Hayes, who was visiting his mother in the neighborhood. "Then I looked up and saw a bunch of sandbags get blown off the levee, and the water come rushing through."

Two days later, the River Des Peres

▶ OVERFLOWED

South St. Louis' streets runneth over July 19. As crest predictions rose throughout the summer, brigades of volunteers piled on more sandbags — but the River Des Peres kept rising to top them.

Jerry Naunheim Jr.

▶ **July 14:**

In St. Louis, city workers start marking the neighborhoods that would need to be evacuated in case the Mississippi rises to 46 feet. They'll do a lot more marking in coming weeks.

▶ **July 15:**

Rain lifts the Mississippi at St. Louis past 43.23 feet, the record crest of 1973. The Missouri River floods U.S. Highway 63, Jefferson City's link to Columbia.

▶ **July 16:**

Emergency officials urge more than 1,000 families in the Carondelet neighborhood to evacuate as water nears the top of the River Des Peres levee.

The levee blows in West Quincy, Mo., shutting down the Bayview Bridge and cutting off the only remaining span open across the Mississippi in the 212-mile stretch of the river from St. Louis to Burlington, Iowa.

Another Missouri River levee goes near St. Charles, flooding farmland and sending 700 more residents to higher ground. The St. Charles levee breach combines the Mississippi and Missouri rivers 20 miles upstream from where they used to meet.

▶ **July 17:**

Clinton, Gore and governors from flooded states meet in Arnold.

A levee collapses in Maryland Heights, reclaiming Creve Coeur Lake and flooding lowlands.

In the midst of the summer's first heat warning, 2,000 sandbaggers work along the River Des Peres to raise the barriers there to 47 feet.

smashed through a half-mile section of sandbags, flooding more homes to their porches and forcing the Missouri National Guard to rescue stranded residents.

Downtown stood dry on a bluff. But the flood wall that shielded low parts of the city started creaking. In mid-July, the bloated Mississippi gouged a hole under the flood wall in north St. Louis and actually shifted the wall a couple of inches. Engineers plugged the hole with 111 cubic feet of concrete and 6,000 tons of rock.

Weird debris — 70 bundles of cut lumber and at least seven propane tanks — floated downstream and nudged the flood wall.

As the rivers flexed toward their crests at the end of July, they pounded the St. Louis area relentlessly.

On July 30, highway engineers finally surrendered to floodwater and closed three major bridges — the McKinley, the Lewis and the Clark. Those closures snarled traffic into some of the worst jams in St. Louis history.

That morning, officials cleared 5,000 employees and residents out of Chesterfield Valley, a high-tech business zone along the Missouri. St. Louis County guards hustled 450 inmates out of a jail in the valley; some of them ended up in another county building — a recreation complex.

The levee guarding the valley would hold, officials said. But, just in case . . .

The levee failed. The Missouri poured into the valley that night, swallowing a 4,000-acre swath in several feet of water, engulfing the jail, covering an airport and closing the Daniel Boone Bridge and Interstate 64. The breach swamped a water plant and flooded a sewage treatment plant, which let raw sewage from 75,000 homes pour into the Missouri.

In south St. Louis the same night, the Mississippi lifted dozens of propane tanks from their berths at a tank yard on the riverfront, ripping the straps that held them down. Fire officials feared that the pipes linking the tanks would snap, spewing a cloud of explosive gas into the air. "That would be the source of a major explosion," said Jim Brady, a spokesman for county police. "If ignited, it could knock down brick walls up to a mile away."

Jerry Naunheim Jr.

▶ **WISHFUL**

A painted sentiment north of the Missouri Botanical Garden proves that citizens of the city's high and dry center are thinking of residents to the north and south of its flood wall.

▼ TENUOUS TIE

Its covered gangways awash to the roofs, the Alton Belle Casino gambling boat relies on a long, makeshift walkway to one of the city's dry spots. Although the boats couldn't cruise, bettors kept the slot machines jingling on the Belle and other area gambling boats.

▶ SLOGGING

Jane Zimmerli watches her step as she helps move belongings from her husband's aunt's home on Hurck Street in south St. Louis.

▼ BREAKAWAY

A towboat pushes a piece of the Spirit of the River barge complex back upstream to its berth. The cresting Mississippi tore the cluster of barges from the city's riverfront, whirled them downstream and smashed them into the piers of the city's largest bridge.

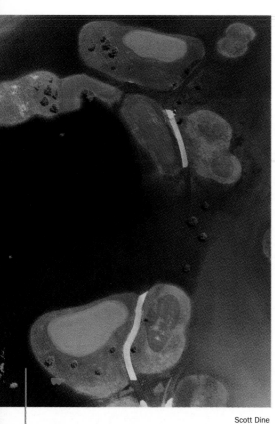

▶ WATER HAZARD

In early July, Sunset Lakes Golf Course already had more brown than greens. The course is southwest of the city near the Meramec River.

Over the next two days, officials cleared almost 12,000 people from south St. Louis and Lemay. Most had no time to pack or grab their pets.

Throughout the day on July 31, television stations broadcast shaky live footage of police rescuing people from rooftops in Chesterfield Valley. Residents who feared that the water supply was about to be lost swarmed into groceries and cleaned the shelves of bottled water.

In Bellefontaine Neighbors in north St. Louis County, the Maline Creek washed over a sandbag wall. "We're losing the battle," a police officer said.

On Aug. 1, the Mississippi muscled into downtown Alton, closed the water plant and punched upward through streets, buckling them under residents' feet.

"I was talking eye to eye with this guy," said Mark Hook, the owner of the flooded Time Out Lounge. "And in five seconds I grew about a foot."

Late that night, the Mississippi captured a barge complex from the St. Louis riverfront and sent it spinning downstream. As the complex broke apart, one of the barges smashed into the piers of the Poplar Street Bridge, the main bridge in downtown St. Louis.

The next day, St. Louisans learned that the worst had passed, that the Mississippi was receding. A reporter asked meteorologist Bill Wipfler if the river might rise again, and he answered with something approaching a prayer.

"No," Wipfler said. "No. No. No."

LANE CLOSINGS ◀

At the flood's peak, a levee break submerges a chunk of Highway 40 (Interstate 64) severing one of the metropolitan area's major traffic arteries.

Jerry Naunheim Jr.

LAST LAUGH

Guidry's Cajun Restaurant keeps a sense of humor even as the River Des Peres attempts to eat the establishment's words.

Jerry Naunheim Jr.

▼
BEFRIENDED

Jim Hirth of the Animal Rescue Team comforts Tina, a guard dog rescued from Sachs Electric Co. on Chesterfield Airport Road.

REROUTED ◀

A bus stop at Carondelet and Waddell avenues in Lemay marks a submerged street corner.

Wes Paz

▼
IMPASSE

A woman finds her path blocked on Marceau Avenue in south St. Louis.

48

▶ **ENTHRALLED**

Wearied sandbaggers and tourists alike come to a bluff above Alton to gaze in awe at the Mississippi's breadth. As the flood wore on, gawkers on highways became a traffic hazard.

A current stronger than commerce

About a dozen of the 485 businesses in Chesterfield Valley stocked up in late July on a new commodity: sandbags.

Few people — very few — believed that the levee protecting the valley would yield to the Missouri River. It had, after all, withstood the river for decades. But business owners stacked a few sandbags around their doors in case some water dribbled through.

"If it breaks, we'll have some protection," said Bob Wood of the camera manufacturer Kalimar Inc., where 75 tons of sandbags shielded the doorways. "If it did happen and we didn't do anything, we'd be scorning ourselves."

But when the levee broke, a *thousand* tons of sandbags wouldn't have guarded Kalimar or the other businesses.

The Missouri smashed through the levee about 10:15 p.m. on July 30, and murky, debris-laden water gushed into the 4,000-acre valley. It flooded manufacturers, consulting firms, restaurants, a pet-supply store and the Spirit of St. Louis Airport.

After the breach, some business owners fought on, futilely, into the following day.

"We had plans A, B, C, D, E — and F, which stands for forget it," said Thom Sehnert, owner of the Smoke House Market. "We went to F about 10 a.m., when the water was 10 feet deep in our store."

In tears, business owners saw the devastation when dawn broke. Trees had snagged a twin-engine jet that the flood had lifted. Cars were submerged to their roofs. Propane tanks bobbed in the water. And files, equipment, tools and dreams were drowned.

In a few days, St. Louis understood the true dimensions of the calamity:

Renyold Ferguson

▶ **STALLED**

Multicolored barges wait out the water across the Mississippi from Portage des Sioux.

Business owners had been so certain of the levee's strength that almost none of them had bought flood insurance.

"Some will never recover," said St. Louis County Executive Buzz Westfall.

The break in the Chesterfield levee was but one battle in the river's summer-long war on businesses.

Throughout the flood zone, water engulfed thousands of businesses or slammed shut the roads leading to them. The flood drowned big chemical companies, railroads, manufacturing firms, tiny family-owned groceries and

a catfish farm. It killed tourism in towns that rely on visitors. It pinched deliveries by submerging hundreds of miles of rail lines and stalling thousands of barges for weeks.

Stalled barges alone cost Missouri and Illinois $100 million a month; estimates of the overall cost of the flood throughout the Midwest ranged from $10 billion to $15 billion.

The owners represented only a small part of the people smacked by the floods. In the St. Louis area, 10,700 people — one out of every 111 workers

Wes Paz

▶ SWAMPED

The receding Mississippi reveals its former power in the positions of two tanker trucks near Highway 367 east of West Alton. A farmer had moved the vehicles to what he thought was high ground.

— lost their jobs for at least a day. Some lost their jobs for months.

The Chesterfield breach drubbed Pohlman Inc., a manufacturing company, meaning that its 250 employees would be out of work for days or weeks. "Counting their family members, there are probably 750 people who depend upon us for a paycheck," said Bob Hoffman, a co-owner. "And those jobs just washed right out the door."

Some businesses persevered. When the flood closed access roads, some firms — especially utilities — took employees

to work in special commuter vehicles: boats and helicopters. Mary Lou and Joe Harrison, who both worked at a Union Electric Co. plant in Portage des Sioux, saw each other only when their boats passed on the Mississippi.

Meanwhile, gamblers on boats up and down the Mississippi kept slot machines humming, reminding some people of Nero fiddling while Rome burned.

"Why not?" asked one gambler. "Is it going to stop people from going to work? No."

Chronology:

▶ **July 18:**

The River Des Peres blows open a 15-foot section of sandbags east of Alabama Avenue and sends more water into the Carondelet neighborhood. Later in the evening, two more chunks of the levee collapse, flooding even more homes.

The break swamps the Monsanto Co.'s Carondelet Plant in south St. Louis.

Health officials warn that the next assault might be a wave of floodwater mosquitoes.

▶ **July 19:**

The owner of Gateway Western Railway, a railroad based in Fairview Heights, says a levee breach near Glasgow has undercut a railroad bed — and that fact might obliterate the railroad.

Floodwater buckles part of Carondelet Boulevard east of Interstate 55.

Monsanto Co. employees tour the plant in boats.

▶ **July 20:**

In the midst of a 2-inch rainstorm, the River Des Peres sweeps away a half mile-long section of sandbags along Germania between Gravois Avenue and Morganford Road, flooding dozens more homes.

▶ **July 21:**

The Mississippi severs the water supply to the Menard Correctional Center in Chester, Ill., leaving 2,450 inmates with no way to shower or flush toilets.

Officials in St. Charles County discover that the flooded Missouri River has scoured away a 100-foot section of highway.

Kevin Manning

▶ BLINDSIDED

Ralph Large, a director of the flooded Chesterfield Bank, confers with the Coast Guard through the bank's shattered windows and soaked vertical blinds.

Larry Williams

▼ SOAKED *(Preceding pages)*

Missouri river floodwater rests in the truck bays of Chesterfield businesses the morning after the Missouri River burst through the Monarch levee.

Jerry Naunheim Jr.

▶ WATERLOGGED

Kevin and Tracy Mueller survey damages to their business, Mueller Bros. Timber Inc. in Old Monroe.

Larry Williams

Larry Williams

SNAGGED ◄

*Floodwater scooped up two
planes that were used for
salvage parts at a
Chesterfield airport and
docked them in a treetop.*

Gary Bohn

▶ **GINGERLY**

*Kathy Nevills makes her way across the remains
of a levee with supplies for the temporary
quarters of Lemay Bank and Trust Co.*

Kevin Manning
▼
SENTRIES

(Following pages)
*Brothers Dennis and Dale
Felts keep watch on the state
of sandbags barring the
Missouri from Trio Motors in
St. Charles.*

Torn down, danced over, and laughed at

Half a day later, Michael R. Frost's voice still quavered when he described how an explosion of water through a levee had nearly squashed him.

"It was gurgling, like the sound a bathtub makes when you pull the plug," said Frost, a marina owner who lives in Lincoln County, Mo. "It was like a vacuum sucking the water. I ran to my road crossing, and the levee blew. It sucked out all the trees — 100-year-old trees that are so thick I couldn't even get my arms around them."

In the flood of 1993, rivers demolished levees with the ease and imagination of a child toying with ant hills. Floodwater tunneled under, crept over, poked through or crawled past levees hundreds of times. Or, as happened when Michael Frost ran for his life, water blasted them open with the force of a bomb.

In all, more than 1,000 of the 1,500 or so levees in the Midwest flood zone fell to the rivers that summer — a failure rate of almost 70 percent. Lamented Jim Brown of the Army Corps of Engineers: "It's not as manageable a thing as anybody would like to believe."

Levees — or dikes — are civilization's most common defense against flooding, and the simplest. Take a mound of earth, rock or clay. Shape it like a dam, fatter at the bottom than the top, and string it between the river and what you want to protect.

If all goes well, the levee will block the water from rushing over your field and into your home. The problem is this: Your neighbors won't like it very much. All that water that would have flooded your land will now flood theirs. So over the years, in the river-dwellers' equivalent of an arms race, levees beget more levees.

In this flood, the rivers hit the levees with such force and soaked them for so long that they failed in all the ways levees can.

Often, a levee's failure was as spectacular as it was horrifying.

From a high point near Columbia, Ill., farmer Virgil Gummersheimer watched the morning of Aug. 1 as the Mississippi crashed through a levee. The river knocked over his grain bins, crushed his barn and smashed his home to splinters.

"It reclaimed its valley," Gummersheimer said.

That wasn't all. That levee breach let the Mississippi claim Valmeyer — a town of 900 founded in 1904 by Swiss farmers and German railroaders — and a 20-mile swath of farmland and hamlets.

In Perry County, Mo., the Mississippi punched through a levee while Army Corps of Engineers worker Harold Smith was nearby in his pickup truck. "There was a big boom, and the water started gushing," said co-worker Carl Raines. "I saw the truck topple over the levee, and the headlights went straight up in the air. I thought he was a goner."

Rescuers found Smith, bruised, dazed and alive, where the river dumped him — a mile away.

At Kaskaskia Island, Ill., a whirlpool in the river signaled that water was rushing into a hole it had burrowed underneath a levee — a sign of imminent collapse. An inspector described the scene over the phone to the corps' natural disaster chief, Jake Scanlon.

"He said, 'What should we do?' " Scanlon said. "And I said, 'Get out of there!' By then, everyone was going. I think I was just reinforcing what they were already doing."

The levee collapsed in seconds. The island, which was settled by French explorers in 1703 and was home to Illinois' first state capitol, was overwhelmed.

Sometimes, the river assaulted a levee quietly, by nibbling away at the ground underneath or by soaking a stack of sandbags on top. Like a sand castle that gets too wet, a sandbag can handle only so much water before it gives way.

In Greene County in Illinois, the Illinois River climbed above an earthen levee and was restrained only by sandbags that workers had piled along the top of the levee — restrained for a while. "It's very doubtful it'll be able to make it," said corps hydrologist Gary Dyhouse.

He was right. Five days later, the river charged through the sandbags and flooded 10,000 acres.

Scott Dine

▶ RIPTIDE

The Mississippi drives a wedge of water through the Fountain Creek levee just north of the Illinois town of Valmeyer. Residents, National Guard troops and volunteers had fought for 24 days to reinforce it.

The rivers may have had help in destroying one levee. In Marion County, Mo., the sheriff investigated allegations that vandals had knocked away a few sandbags, allowing the Mississippi to flood 15,000 acres of farmland.

"It's mind-boggling," said Sheriff Dan Campbell. "Some sandbags are pulled, and you've got millions of dollars in damage."

And sometimes the levees worked.

In St. Louis, Hannibal, Ste.

Genevieve, Kimmswick, Cape Girardeau, Canton and other Missouri towns, levees and flood walls held, even though they were saturated and riddled with holes.

"I feel relieved, a little bit numb," said Jesse Franks, Canton's mayor. "It's like when we used to come back from the battles in World War II. You're happy you're still here, but you don't let it loose."

Chronology:

▶ **July 22:**
Just upriver from Chester, the Mississippi River smashes through a 52-foot levee around Kaskaskia Island. The river covers the island as residents struggle to retrieve their belongings and their livestock.

▶ **July 23:**
Four boys and two adult counselors drown when a flash flood catches them in a cave at Cliff Cave Park in south St. Louis County.

▶ **July 25:**
Floodwater rushing through a levee in Perry County, Mo., pushes a Corps of Engineers worker about a mile. "You can imagine what kind of ride that was," a colleague says.

▶ **July 30:**
The Missouri River breaks through a levee guarding the Chesterfield Valley. Within hours, almost 500 businesses, a jail and a stretch of Interstate 64 are awash in 8 feet of water.

Highway officials close the Lewis and Clark bridges.

In south St. Louis, the Mississippi lifts propane tanks off their mounts and threatens to cause leaks that would spew explosive gas into the air. Residents within a half-mile are cleared out.

Residents move back to Canton, Mo., after beating the flood.

▶ **July 31:**
Engineers pump 111 cubic yards of concrete into a hole under St. Louis' flood wall.

Hundreds of Jefferson County residents pack in Kimmswick and in Arnold, where levees are close to collapsing.

▶ ENGULFED

(Pages 60/61)

The Mississippi widens into the flood plain of Monroe County, Ill.

▼

RAPIDS

The rain-swollen North River blasts over a levee at Highway 61 near Palmyra, Mo., July 3. It was one of the state's first levees to fail.

OVERRUN ▼

The Mississippi wins again at a levee near Winfield, Mo., July 3.

GAINING GROUND ▼

Water from the Mississippi fans out over a farm near Columbia, Ill., after a levee break.

BEACON

The pitched roof and steeple of Immaculate Conception Catholic Church are among the few discernible structures after the flooding of Kaskaskia Island in Illinois.

▶ AWASH

The sun illuminates the current of the Mississippi flowing through a residential area of Valmeyer. The town of about 900 last flooded in 1947, before a levee was built.

▶ LESSON

The roof of Valmeyer Community High School seems to float Aug. 2 after a levee break flooded the town.

REACHING ◀

The river spared Valmeyer's Union Pacific railroad tracks — barely; and for no one knew how long.

Wayne Crosslin

PERSEVERING

Workers fight the rain and the river to reinforce and raise the levee protecting homes near the River Des Peres.

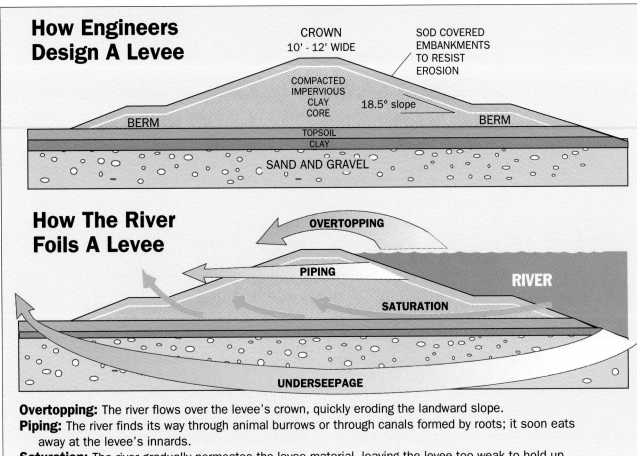

How Engineers Design A Levee

CROWN
10' - 12' WIDE

SOD COVERED
EMBANKMENTS
TO RESIST
EROSION

COMPACTED
IMPERVIOUS
CLAY
CORE

18.5° slope

BERM

BERM

TOPSOIL

CLAY

SAND AND GRAVEL

How The River Foils A Levee

OVERTOPPING

PIPING

RIVER

SATURATION

UNDERSEEPAGE

Overtopping: The river flows over the levee's crown, quickly eroding the landward slope.

Piping: The river finds its way through animal burrows or through canals formed by roots; it soon eats away at the levee's innards.

Saturation: The river gradually permeates the levee material, leaving the levee too weak to hold up its own weight.

Underseepage: The river pushes through a loose layer of sand beneath the levee and breaks through the ground on the other side, weakening the ground the levee sits on.

Source: Army Corps of Engineers

Post-Dispatch Graphic By Chuck Groth

Jim Rackwitz

▶ **IMPERILED**

Ste. Genevieve huddles under the protection of its levee July 20, weeks before the Mississippi's crest. Volunteers kept nighttime vigils along its levee for weeks, and the town that claims to be the oldest west of the river escaped much damage.

Gary Bohn

▶ BLOCKADED

*Two counties south of St. Louis on the Illinois side of the Mississippi,
Prairie du Rocher residents build a rock and sandbag levee to close
one open spot in the town's defenses.*

Kevin Manning

▶ **PREPARED**

A sandbag wall wraps around a home on the outskirts of Prairie du Rocher before the levee break.

Fighting water with water

Sweating, grunting, hefting sandbag after sandbag, hundreds of workers struggled throughout the summer to reinforce a levee shielding one of Illinois' oldest towns from the Mississippi River. But by late July, it seemed certain that the Mississippi would foil the work and crash through the levee.

"That's the worst part," said Wayne Reinking, principal of the elementary school in Prairie du Rocher. "Until the last few days, it was if it's going to break. Now, it's when."

Reinking and his co-workers didn't know it yet, but the Mississippi wouldn't break the levee.

The people would.

French explorers founded Prairie du Rocher in 1722 in rich bottomland four miles east of the Mississippi. Some of the trappers and traders moved upstream and built a town they named St. Louis.

Today, about 700 people live in Prairie du Rocher, some of them descendants of those first explorers. The town serves as a commercial center for the farmers who work the fields nearby.

As the flood charged through the Midwest in 1993, people in Prairie du Rocher grew increasingly worried about the two levees protecting their town.

The first levee — called the primary levee — ran for 20 miles along the Mississippi. The second levee, a shorter one called a flank levee, ran east and west along the north side of Prairie du Rocher. Imagine the two levees as a

Chronology:

▶ **Aug. 1:**

The Mississippi breaches the levee at Columbia, Ill., smashing a home to bits and engulfing Valmeyer, population 900. Water begins crawling toward Prairie du Rocher.

The Mississippi floods a dozen businesses in downtown Alton, closes the water plant and lifts the streets.

On the riverfront, the Mississippi snatches a barge complex and carries it downstream. From 9 a.m. to 10 a.m., the river tops out at 49.58 feet, more than six feet above the old record and more than 19 feet above flood stage.

▶ **Aug. 2:**

St. Louis officials expand the evacuation area around the propane tank. All told, 11,800 people are cleared out, including the residents of a nursing home. One man stayed. "I'm 80 years old," he tells officials. "If it's going to get me, it's going to get me."

▶ **Aug. 3:**

In Prairie du Rocher, workers open a 400-foot section of the Mississippi levee, a last-ditch effort to save the town. "There's no guarantee it's going to work," said hydrologist Gary Dyhouse.

▶ **Aug. 4:**

The hole is too small, so workers dig and blast the gouge to 1,000 feet. It might be working.

▶ **Aug. 5:**

About 1,000 volunteers show up to help reinforce the flank levee above Prairie du Rocher; meanwhile, water drains out of the 1,000-foot hole in the main levee. One resident is so confident that he mows his lawn.

The Senate approves $5.8 billion in flood-relief.

Jerry Naunheim Jr.

▶ SCRAMBLING

Near Prairie du Rocher, a barge crane struggles to gouge a large enough hole in a levee to make the Army Corps Of Engineers' last-ditch plan work.

▼ DESPONDENT

Carol DuFrenne mourns the loss of a hand-built home and new machine shed.

Wes Paz

▼ RALLIED *(Preceding pages)*

Sandbaggers stretch out in force to build up Prairie du Rocher's levee in preparation for the Mississippi's crest.

Jerry Naunheim Jr.

capital L, with the river to the left and with the town sitting under the right tip of the shorter arm.

The problem with the primary levee was that it was sopping with river water. Like a rag that has soaked up as much spilled milk as it can, the levee was beginning to ooze. And the river was reaching underneath, clawing holes through the earth.

Everyone in town knew that if that first levee failed near the town, the floodwater rushing through could overwhelm the second one.

So, for a while, the town tried to reinforce both levees. Then, on Aug. 1, the Mississippi did something that few people had expected. It punched a hole in the primary levee far from Prairie du Rocher, about 20 miles upstream, at the top of the L.

What that meant was simple and terrifying: An unstoppable avalanche of water 15 feet high was rushing toward the flank levee — and the town. And it would get there in about a day.

The residents cleared out, leaving a ghost town. Only a few volunteers, National Guard soldiers and a handful of workers from the Army Corps of Engineers stayed behind.

"It's getting really scary," said Nichole Ray, who stuck around to feed the workers.

Local leaders and the corps agreed on a desperate plan: They would fight water with water. They would tear a hole in the primary levee, near the elbow of the L.

The hole, they hoped, would do two things. First, it would create a "backflood," a wall of water that would cushion the impact of the coming avalanche and protect the flank levee.

Second, it would allow some of the water pouring in from the north to drain out, as if the valley were a 20-mile bucket and they were drilling a hole in the bottom.

"It's the only thing we could think of to make the difference between losing Prairie du Rocher and saving Prairie du Rocher," said Gary Dyhouse, a Corps of Engineers hydrologist. "The government usually takes two or three years to do an engineering study.

"We didn't have that luxury."

Within hours of the break upriver,

Wes Paz

▶ **VOYAGERS**

Striking coal miners paddle away from the levee at Prairie du Rocher, where they were delivering sandbags to isolated parts of the levee.

workers climbed aboard cranes and used clamshell diggers to scoop out a 400-foot break in the levee.

It wasn't big enough.

The backflood blunted the impact of the big wave, but the combined flow from the accidental and the intentional breaks started filling the valley, threatening to slosh over the flank levee.

The next day, workers tried a less delicate approach to widening the drain hole: dynamite. Against the advice of engineers, who said the dynamite could set off a chain reaction that would topple the entire levee, they touched off two blasts.

"It was such a critical situation, we didn't have any choice," said Dan Reitz, chairman of the Randolph County Board of Commissioners.

When they realized that the dynamite wasn't gouging big enough holes, the workers returned to the clamshell

digger. They scooped a hole 1,000 feet long. Meanwhile, other crews stacked sandbags and truckload after truckload of rock on the flank levee to strengthen it.

Within a day, the water started dropping in the valley, sliding away from the flank levee. The end of the story: Prairie stayed dry.

That didn't console Carol DuFrenne and other people whose homes north of the flank levee were swamped. The wall of water rushing south would have flooded their homes, even without the man-made backflood nearby. But the inevitability of their losses made them no less painful.

"We had a beautiful home, fireplace wall to wall, a nice new machine shed," Carol DuFrenne said between muffled sobs. "And we put in every nail ourselves."

Jerry Naunheim Jr.

▶ **EVICTED**

*Joan Gust of Portage des Sioux learns that the
Mississippi will continue to rise, forcing her to
leave her home.*

Living in
Nowhere Land

T he backyard fence was the bor-
derline, Sylvester Freed declared.

Time after time, Freed, 84, predicted
that the Mississippi River would respect
that boundary of the home he shared

with his wife and her sister in St. Peters.
The river normally flowed six miles
from the house, and in the 60 years
they'd lived there, it had never spread
beyond the fence.

But by July 15, Freed could look
from the kitchen window and see the

L.T. Spence

▼
HOLDOUT

*Reed Bauer, 82, finally accepts a ride from
Coast Guardsmen and becomes another of
northern St. Charles County's evacuees.*

Chronology:

▶ **Aug. 6:**

The Mississippi's crest — its
high point — rolls past Ste.
Genevieve without
demolishing the town's levee.
"I feel almost in a holiday
mood today," says Mayor Bill
Anderson.

St. Charles County officials
say inspectors will look at
flood-damaged homes before
residents can move back in.

The House approves the
flood-aid bill.

▶ **Aug. 7:**

Analysts say the flood
affected 10,700 jobs in the
St. Louis area, meaning that
one out of every 111 workers
was out of work for at least a
day.

A group called World Vision
says it will coordinate
cleanup volunteers in the St.
Louis area.

▶ **Aug. 8:**

Fifty-two elderly and sick
residents of the Community
Care Center of Lemay return
to the home after the
evacuation order is lifted.

The worst has passed. The
Mississippi crest sweeps
past Cairo, Ill., and into the
lower Mississippi River,
where the wider channel can
handle more water.

river lap, lap, lapping at the fence. Within a week, the river pushed into the home, evicting Freed, his wife, Edna, 85, and her sister, Marie, 83.

In six days, the river had done something that old age and poor health couldn't do. It had stripped the three of their home — and their independence.

As the floodwater advanced across the Midwest, it stole homes from thousands of families. In the St. Louis area alone, the flood evicted 25,000 people. Some were gone for days, some for weeks and some for months. Hundreds would never return: The flood had ground their homes to scrap lumber.

For some, a police officer's knock at the door before dawn warned them that they'd have to leave. For others, it was the blare of a civil service siren. And for a handful, it was the sound of rushing water.

The result was usually the same: The victims clutched a few belongings and let the water claim whatever furniture, clothes and family treasures they hadn't had the foresight — or the pessimism — to have moved to higher ground.

"There was a woman, 50-52 years old, who came in here holding the hand of her 5 or 6-year-old granddaughter," said Clyde Miller, who worked at a Salvation Army Shelter. "She said, 'This is all I have left.' Her clothing, her furniture, the little girl's toys were all gone.

"It can bring tears to your eyes. There are stories like that every day, every hour."

Some refugees crowded into bedrooms, living rooms or garages of friends or relatives, where tight quarters rubbed nerves raw.

"Two families together under the same roof, it just don't work," said Terry Welch, who moved with her husband to a relative's two-bedroom trailer in Wright City. "Sometimes, just to get some privacy, my husband and I get into our old truck and drive around awhile, drinking coffee and puffing on old stogies."

Some fled to motels, tents, recreational vehicles or one of the dozens of American Red Cross or Salvation Army shelters. In the shelters, the refugees found a gentle touch.

"You figure there have to be people worse off than you," said Kathy Lutes, who moved to a shelter from a trailer

Larry Williams

▶ **CLEARING OUT**

Chris DeSherlia of Grafton prepares to move to higher ground, piling his belongings on the Great River Road, July 10.

home in West Alton. "But the people here, they make you feel good.

"They must be well-trained. Either that, or it's from the heart.

"I think it's from the heart."

But whether the victims drifted to shelters, motel rooms or friends' homes, uncertainty haunted them. When could they move back home? *Could* they?

When the flood shoved Linda and Tom Lupo and their two children from their mobile home and into a 14-by-16-foot motel room, it shoved them into a life without privacy or luxuries and almost without hope.

"It's tough for a lot of people, and I know others are worse off," said Tom Lupo. "But I'm worried where we'll be in two or three months."

Sitting motionless on a motel room bed, boxed in by her family and their clothes, toiletries, toys and food, Linda Lupo spoke for thousands: "We've stuck it out here in nowhere land, not knowing what will happen next."

Gary Bohn

WAITING ◀

Tom Wright prepares for the flood by hoisting appliances to the ceiling of his St. Louis basement.

Karen Elshout

STRESS RELIEF ◀

Loretta Goehring hugs Sam Chapman on the sandbag line in flood-threatened Kimmswick, July 8. Goehring feared that Chapman would make himself ill helping his daughter move belongings out of her trailer in the hot, muggy weather.

▼ RIVER VIEW

Jim Lenk peeks into his flooded garage in Old Monroe in late July.

Jerry Naunheim Jr.

MESSENGERS

Fireman Eric Thomas, left, and police officer Randy Sasenger make a stop on their door-to-door tour of south St. Louis. They told Mary and Joseph LoCigno that they might have to evacuate their home near the River Des Peres.

411

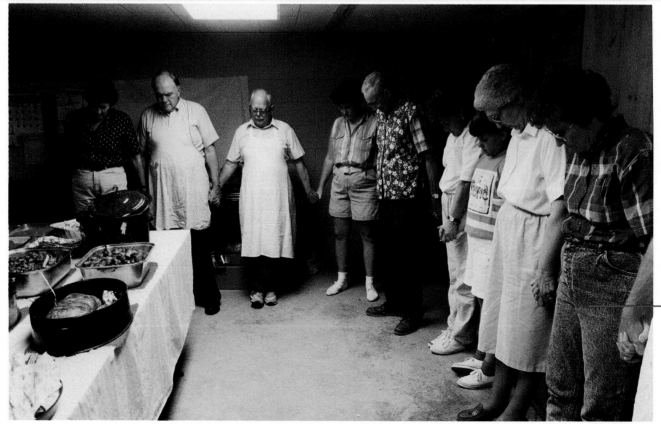

Jerry Naunheim Jr.

Coffins that the Missouri River lifted out of a cemetery in Hardin, Mo., come to rest on flood-damaged Missouri Route 10. The river moved 756 of the cemetery's 1,544 dead.

REVERENT

Members of the First Christian Church of Bowling Green say a grace before serving dinner to flood victims gathered at Ramsey Creek Baptist Church Aug. 21.

Larry Williams

▶ ONE WAY *(Pages 82/83)*

Kim Gillman, his wife Jeanna and their dog leave West Alton via the only dry way out of town on July 8: the Burlington Northern Railroad tracks.

SHELTERED ◀

Jackie Wright, left, and her aunt, Marie Wright, wait for help at Cleveland Naval Junior ROTC High School, one of the many shelters for evacuees. They hold Marie Wright's two children, Amanda, 10 months, and Jonathan, 2.

Wes Paz

▼ CROWDED

Linda Lupo and her family pack into a hotel room in St. Charles in August. They had been out of their home for a month.

Karen Elshout

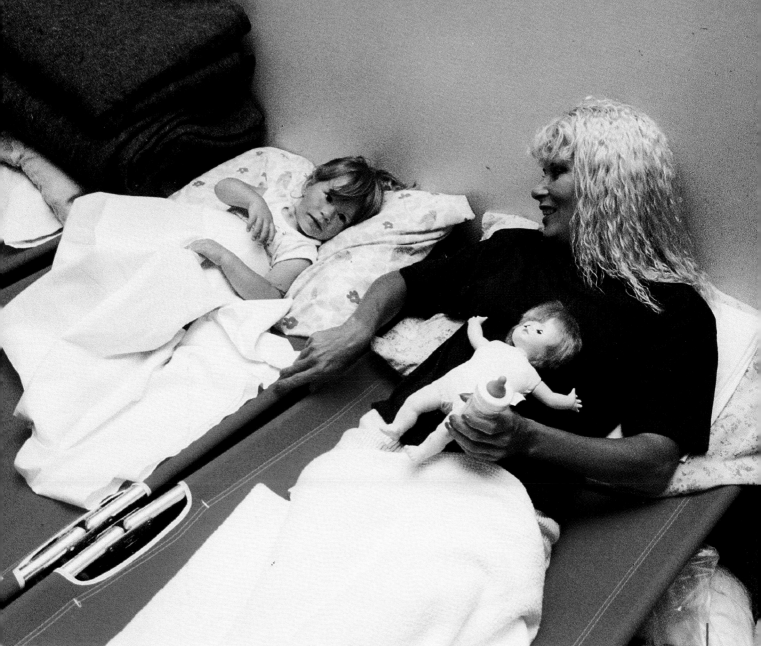

Wendi Fitzgerald

Gary Bohn

BEDTIME ◄

Vickie Chandler and her daughter Megan Odle, 2, share a story in a shelter in Spanish Lake.

▼
FOUND

Joyce Cox reunites with her two cats, Gizzard and Squeaks, after Humane Society officials rescued them from Cox's house in south St. Louis. Many who were evacuated because of the risk of a propane explosion had to leave pets behind, and were told they would be gone only a short while.

▶ **BUOYANT**

Marty Sontheimer steps into the floodwater just outside his St. Charles County home, where he spelled out his reaction to the flood.

Karen Elshout

We shall not be moved

Nothing was going to kick Edwin and Ruth Macarthy out of their home. Nothing.

Not hell.

Not high water.

Hell left them alone in the summer of 1993. But high water worked like the devil to chase the Macarthys from Lemay in south St. Louis County. Long after their neighbors had fled the threat of the bloated River Des Peres, the Macarthys stayed put behind a wall of sandbags 13 feet high.

"It's like a bunker," said Ed Macarthy, a retired firefighter with a jaw like a shelf of granite. "When you look out the window, you don't see anything but sandbags unless you get up on the second floor."

Said Ruth Macarthy: "You probably think we're crazy, don't you?"

In the flood of 1993, defiant ones like the Macarthys waged personal war against the rivers. They used muscle, sandbags, pumps and plywood. Whether they won or lost, their tenacity in the teeth of disaster captured the attention of America.

■

"NO FEAR."

That's how Marty Sontheimer of St. Charles County greeted the flood. His cedar-wrapped home became an island, but his message shouted from the rooftop. Using white sandbags, Sontheimer spelled out the loud antithesis of an SOS.

"We'd all worked our butts off for three or four days, and I just got tired of it," Sontheimer said. "Everybody was getting all worried about the flood. I was just kind of telling everybody, 'Hey, don't worry.' If you're going to worry about it, you're just going to get gray."

■

Elsewhere in St. Charles County, Tim Smith was the last man to leave his neighborhood on July 16.

And his boat wouldn't start.

When a fire department boat offered him a lift, Smith yelled: "I'm not leaving my dogs!"

Giving up on his stalled motor, Smith loaded his boat with belongings and paddled for the levee, where his friend Dennis Harper waited.

"I've got to get my animals — three dogs and a cat," Smith said, as he handed Harper a pink pillowcase and a half dozen plastic trash bags full of clothes, food and utensils. "We need a box for the cat; she'll go berserk in the boat."

Harper climbed aboard with Smith, and they paddled back to the flooded

Wayne Crosslin

DAILY CONSTITUTIONAL ◀

Longtime Portage des Sioux resident Moe Boschert goes for a wade to the town's temporary post office.

Chronology:

▶ **Aug. 9:**

Two Missouri National Guard sandbaggers get married.

▶ **Aug. 10:**

In Portage des Sioux, flood victims carry on, even in a flooded town. "Some are cleaning out the fire hall," said Ray Tubbesing, the town's fire chief. "Some are over there in the nuns' home. Some are working on the water plant, trying to get that back in service."

▶ **Aug. 11:**

Near what was once Valmeyer, residents are living in a tent city.

▶ **Aug. 12:**

In St. Louis County, Clinton signs the flood-aid bill.

▶ **Aug. 15:**

World Vision holds a rally to start clean-up efforts. About 1,500 people show up.

Weather experts issue this warning: The ground is so saturated that the area should expect more flooding in the fall and next year.

house, where they retrieved the animals.

"I've seen a lot of monsoons in my time, but I've never seen water come up like this," Smith said. "But I didn't have a home for my animals. They don't have anybody else, and I love them too much."

In south St. Louis and in Lemay, police pleaded with residents to flee from the flooded River Des Peres and from the threat of a propane explosion. Sometimes, people chose to leave before police told them to.

"And in some cases," said police Lt. Col. Raymond Lauer, "God is doing the evacuating."

Farmer Gary Iffrig remained on his land, even though the Mississippi River swallowed his family's soybean field and the two-story home his great-grandfather had built.

Iffrig stayed on a dry patch with a companion, Sue Smith, plus a dozen cats, a few chickens and a chocolate-brown Labrador named Spike. Smith and Iffrig slept in a tent — when they weren't chasing off coyotes, spiders, poisonous snakes or bitter memories.

"How can you sleep when your granny's china cabinet is floating down the river or the tires are floating out of the barn?" Iffrig said.

But despite a tornado, storms and the flood, Iffrig stuck with his land.

"It's like sitting with a sick friend," Iffrig said. "You don't leave 'til he gets better — or dies."

Karen Elshout

▶ **ISLAND HOME**

The campsite at which Gary Iffrig and his companion, Sue Smith, stayed for five weeks.

▼ **WATCHMAN**

Gary Iffrig keeps watch over his flooded farmland in St. Charles County, using his shotgun to deal with "snakes and varmints."

Karen Elshout

► **MESSAGE** *(Pages 86 – 87)*

A line written in sandbags marks Marty Sontheimer's home on Iffrig Road in St. Charles County.

DEFIANT

Ed Macarthy checks his crew's handiwork.

► **FORTRESS**

Kevin Macarthy, son of Ed Macarthy, and his uncle Tom Ray stroll toward the Macarthy home that the family barricaded to keep out the flooding River Des Peres.

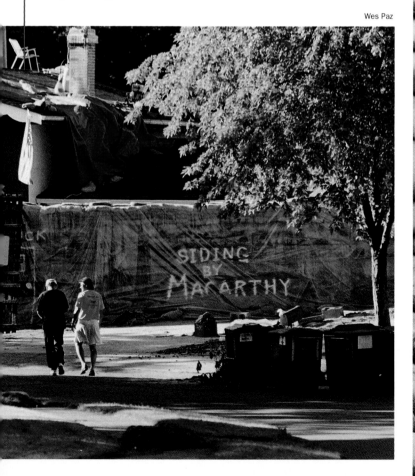

▶ **STUNNED**

Alma McKay reacts to the damage to her home on Davis Street near the River Des Peres. She and her husband had lived there for more than 40 years.

Washed upon the shores

This would be no ordinary cleanup job. "There will be dead fish inside the walls," said Tom Van-Hare, an organizer of the cleanup in the St. Louis area, "algae inside the outlets, snakes in the bath, 1,000 minnows on top of the kitchen table."

And there would be mud, mosquitoes, tires, trees, dead mice, live possums, car parts, catfish, rats, rotting crops, sewage, scrap lumber, shingles, washing machines. There would be garbage, gasoline, propane, paper, pesticides, herbicides, bricks, bacteria, disease-carrying flies — and a sickening stench that would linger for months.

When the water finally retreated, the flood's victims discovered that the rivers had stained some things coffee brown and pasted others with a muck the color of canned peas. And they discovered a pain heavier than the first sting of loss.

"At first you get your adrenaline going and you cope," said Betty Selkowitz, the owner of a flooded lingerie store in Davenport, Iowa. "It's like a nightmare hurrying around to get your things out.

"Then the depression sets in."

Some people found that even if their homes were standing, their furniture

was so poisoned with river water that they could only tear it up and throw it out.

In St. Charles County, building inspectors Robert Boschert and Brian Butts walked through a home that had been flooded. "This is a goner. This is a goner," Boschert said as he pointed to flood-damaged walls and floors. He opened a refrigerator, where shut-off electric lines had let food rot for more than a month. "Whew!" he cried. "That's definitely a goner."

Health officials worried about the long-term effects of the flood. Stagnant pools of water would give mosquitoes

Ted Dargan

▶ COPING

*A woman in Grafton, Ill., prepares a videotape
record of flood damage for her insurance company.*

ideal breeding ground, and flies would swarm to the sewage left behind. The mosquitoes might carry encephalitis, malaria or dengue fever, and the flies might spread diarrheal illnesses. Chemicals and sewage would linger as a powder after the water receded. "People are

going to be breathing contaminated dust," said one federal official.

The cleanup would take billions of dollars — and some professional help.

After some squabbling over how to pay for aid, Congress agreed to spend $5.7 billion to help flood victims, an

amount that officials conceded would barely put a dent in the cost of the damage. President Bill Clinton signed the measure into law in a ceremony in St. Louis County.

As victims started mopping up, the American Red Cross passed out free

Karen Elshout

▶ DISCARDED

An old banjo clock and a family photo top a pile of flood-damaged goods on South Broadway in St. Louis.

STUNNED ▼

Keith and Teresa Ham return to their home in Deerfield Village Mobile Home Park in St. Charles Aug. 3.

Karen Elshout

cleanup kits — brooms, a scrub brush, a mop, a pail, cleaning chemicals and trash bags. More than 15,000 people had picked kits up by mid-August.

In the St. Louis area, a group called World Vision organized cleanup volunteers through churches and promised to donate $3.2 million in cash and supplies. About 1,500 people showed up at the group's first rally.

The Federal Emergency Management Agency, state extension services and local emergency agencies offered advice on how to get rid of stains and smells and on how to stay healthy. The federal agency sent hundreds of people into the field to help people apply for grants and loans and to share advice.

It would take months.

"This is a unique disaster," said Brian McWilliams of the agency. "The flood hit, hit again, hit again and stayed. We never expected that it was going to be for this duration or of this magnitude.

"It was like one disaster after another after another."

STRAINED

Jim Countney hefts a damaged piece of furniture onto a pile outside the This N That Shop on South Broadway.

Karen Elshout

PRICELESS

Many families were evacuated with no time to save irreplaceable family mementos, like this album.

Jerry Naunheim Jr.

To parley with the brown behemoth

When the water finally receded, it left something harder to dispose of than mud, dead fish and driftwood.

It left questions, hundreds of them.

When could people move back to the flood plain? Should they? Should the government buy flooded homes? Should the government reimburse people who had no flood insurance? Should the government rebuild levees? When will the water rise again?

And the biggest question: Why?

Why did the rivers reach so far to flood so many homes, businesses and farms?

To answer that the rivers rose because rain deluged the Midwest only skims the surface. That answer doesn't explain why the water became a disaster.

So some people looked higher for answers, and they saw in the flood the fist of a vengeful god. God sent the flood, they said, to punish St. Louis for allowing riverboat gambling or to punish the nation for allowing abortion.

In that case, others asked, why were the gambling boats and the government still in business? And why were homes of the poor floating downstream?

Some people thought the flood showed that the flood plain needed better protection, with more levees and flood walls, or higher ones. Within weeks after the rivers reached their crest, residents and business owners began calling for federal help to rebuild the broken barriers. By mid-August, the Army Corps of Engineers said it would make repairing the levee in Chesterfield one of its first projects.

Finally, some people also saw in the flood the hand of humanity, but a hand that had done too much, not too little.

"When you get a monster flood like this one, the levee system can actually contribute to the problems," said Kevin Coyle, the head of a river conservation group called American Rivers. The levees give the rivers less room to spread out, thus raising their height when they flood.

"You have to ask the question: After the taxpayers spent $25 billion on this, does it work?"

Some scientists and environmentalists called for a partial return to nature, for humans to remove most of the homes and businesses from the flood plain and allow the rivers some elbow room. They conceded the idea would create a political storm by pitting farmers and developers against conservationists.

"And there are very few politicians who have the spine to take something like that on," said Norm Stucky, a biologist with the Missouri Conservation Department. "But unless something is done, the situation is only going to get worse."

Odell Mitchell Jr.

▶ **UNDER NOAH'S ARCH**

St. Louis' drowned riverfront became an attraction in its own right.

Illinois River

ILLINOIS

ALTON

Mississippi River

MISSOURI

Missouri River

ST. LOUIS | **EAST ST. LOUIS**

Meramec River

KEY TO LANDSAT PHOTOS

0   20 miles

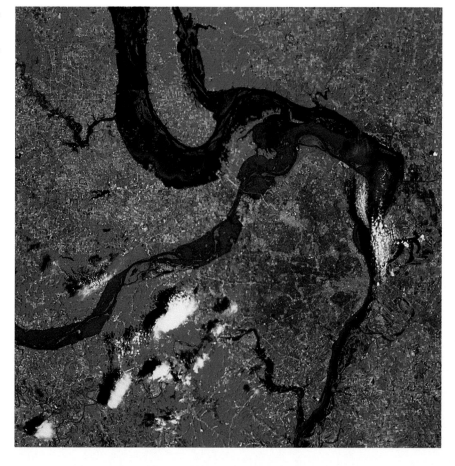

▼ SWOLLEN

LandSat satellite photographs, shot July 4, 1988 (top) and July 18, 1993, reveal the stark contrast between normal summer water levels, and the wide reach of the Mississippi and Missouri rivers near the height of the flood of 1993.

▶ IN COUNTRY

(Back cover)

President Bill Clinton's helicopter sweeps out to survey the flood zone July 17.

J. B. Forbes

Acknowledgments

From late June through late August when the Mississippi and Missouri Rivers were washing over levees and creating havoc in the St. Louis area and in the small towns and rural areas up and down the rivers, the Post-Dispatch was providing its readers with stories, photographs, maps and graphics that would fill several volumes the size of this book. Several pages of each day's edition were taken over with news of The Flood.

Nearly every one of the 284 employees in the Post-Dispatch newsroom contributed in some manner. The newspaper's 18 photographers, under the supervision of director of photography J.B. Forbes, traveled by plane, helicopter, automobile, boat and foot to get the images of the flood. They are credited next to their photographs in this book. The photos are representative of the thousands they took pertaining to The Flood. Virgil Tipton, author of the text of this book, was the lead writer for most days' editions. Metropolitan editor Laszlo Domjan and city editor Tim Bross coordinated the daily coverage. The reporting and writing of Harry Levins, Tim O'Neil and Tom Uhlenbrock were drawn on heavily for this book. Nearly all of the newspaper's reporters, including those from sports, business and features, contributed copy, as did writers from the editorial page. Members of the newspaper's Washington bureau were returned to St. Louis to assist in the coverage. The newsroom's nine artists, under the supervision of news art director Tony Lazorko, were using their computers daily to produce graphics and maps to help explain the ongoing tragedy.

The work in this book is a culmination of the effort of all these newspaper men and women. In addition to those credited above or elsewhere in this book, the following made significant contributions to the newspaper's flood coverage.

William Allen, Courtney Barrett, Harper Barnes, Kim Bell, Donald L. Berns, Christine Bertelson, Kathleen Best, Charles Bosworth Jr., Carolyn Bower, Tom Borgman, Daniel R. Browning, Tim Bryant, Patricia Corrigan, Jim Creighton, John W. Curley, Foster Davis, Sally Bixby Defty, Philip Dine, Geoffrey Dubson, Robert W. Duffy, Ralph Dummit, James Dustin, Linda Eardley, Nordeka English, Donald E. Franklin, Alan Fredman, Margaret Wolf Freivogel, Philip Gaitens, James Gallagher, Terry Ganey.

Ellen Gardner, Patrick E. Gauen, Margaret Gillerman, Adam Goodman, Robert Goodrich, Charlotte Grimes, Thom Gross, Ray Gunter, June Heath, Susan Hegger, Peter Hernon, Virginia Hick, Edward A. Higgins, Joe Holleman, Robert Holt Jr., Repps Hudson, Harry Jackson, Robert Kelly, Carolyn Kingcade, Stephen Kirkland, Marcia L. Koenig, Robert L. Koenig, Edward H. Kohn, Roger Kuechler, Bill Lambrecht, Robert LaRouche, Phyllis Brasch Librach, Fred W. Lindecke, Phil Linsalata, Joan Little, Roy Malone, Jo Mannies, Robert Manor, Dan Martin, Robert W. McCoy, Nancy Miller, Jim Mosley, David Nicklaus, Tim Novak, Lia Nower, Steve Parker, Robert Pastin.

Jan Paul, Gail Pennington, Deborah Peterson, Mark Peterson, Thomas Pettit, Tim Poor, Wendy Rabe, Michael Reilly, Kathleen Richardson, Marianna Riley, Tommy Robertson, Kathryn Rogers, Jon Sawyer, Mark Schlinkmann, Martha Shirk, Roger Signor, Bill Smith, Al Stamborski, Jerri Stroud, Robert Steyer, Vicki Swyers, Joseph Tannian, Susan C. Thomson, Arne Thorbjornson, Theresa Tighe, Cynthia Todd, Carolyn Tuft, Judith VandeWater, Victor Volland, Tat Warner, Richard K. Weil, Richard H. Weiss, Tom Wheatley, Joe Whittington, Lewis Williams, Sue Ann Wood, Lori Teresa Yearwood, Virginia Young, Cindy Zirwes.

▶ **VICTORS**

Residents and a state trooper view a sunset over a dry Prairie du Rocher.

Jerry Naunheim Jr.